HOW TO WIN THE INTERNET AND GO VIRAL

HOW TO WIN THE INTERNET AND GO VIRAL

ELI ROGERS

Eli Rogers

CONTENTS

How To Win The Internet And Go Viral

Chapter 1: Understanding Virality

1. The Anatomy of Viral Content
2. Psychological Triggers and Emotional Responses
3. Case Studies: Sensational Internet Phenomena

Chapter 2: Crafting Resonating Content

1. Identifying Your Niche
2. Understanding Your Audience
3. Mastering the Timing of Posts

Chapter 3: Leveraging Trends for Virality

1. Trendspotting in Social Media
2. Utilizing Trending Topics for Engagement
3. Case Studies: Successful Use of Trends

Chapter 4: Ethical Considerations in Viral Marketing

Chapter 15: Future Trends in Digital Marketing and Virality

1. Predicting Future Social Media Trends
2. Adapting to Changes in Digital Marketing Practices
3. Preparing for the Future of Virality

CHAPTER 1: UNDERSTANDING VIRALITY

The Anatomy of Viral Content

Viral content is an enigma wrapped in the digital behavior of the modern world. It's a blend of art and science, where certain elements come together to create a piece of content that spreads like wildfire across the internet. To understand this phenomenon, we must dissect the components that make up viral content.

Firstly, there's the element of value. Viral content often provides something valuable to its audience, whether it's entertainment, information, or inspiration. This value compels users to share the content with others. For instance, consider how-to videos that exploded in popularity because they offered quick and easy solutions to everyday problems.

Next is relatability. When people see themselves or their experiences reflected in a piece of content, they're more likely to engage with it. Memes are a prime example; their humor often stems from shared experiences or common social observations.

Uniqueness also plays a crucial role in virality. In a sea of constant online noise, unique and original content stands out. The Ice Bucket Challenge gained traction due to its novel approach to charity fundraising by combining philanthropy with an entertaining challenge.

Timing can't be overlooked either. Content released at just the right moment can ride the wave of current events or trends and gain significant attention. A tweet commenting on a major event as it unfolds can quickly become part of the larger conversation.

Emotionally charged content tends to perform well because it creates a strong connection with viewers. Whether it's joy, surprise, anger, or sadness – if it evokes emotion strongly enough for someone to react, it has potential for virality.

Lastly, simplicity and shareability are key factors. If content is too complex or difficult to share, its chances of going viral diminish significantly. The ALS Ice Bucket Challenge was simple: pour ice water over your head, film it, and challenge others.

Understanding these elements helps creators craft content with better odds for virality but remember – there's no guaranteed formula for success in this unpredictable digital landscape.

Psychological Triggers and Emotional Responses

Human psychology plays an integral role in what makes us decide to share online content with our networks. Several psychological triggers

prompt these behaviors by tapping into our emotions and cognitive biases.

One such trigger is social currency – we share things that make us look good in front of our peers. When we find something funny or clever online and pass it along, we're not just sharing a joke; we're signaling our own sense of humor and taste.

Another trigger is storytelling which has been used throughout human history as a means to connect and communicate effectively. Stories evoke emotional responses that can lead to higher engagement rates online because they allow audiences to experience empathy and form personal connections with what they're viewing.

The fear-of-missing-out (FOMO) effect also drives people towards sharing viral content; nobody wants to be left out of what everyone else is talking about. This psychological phenomenon explains why live-tweeting during events or TV shows can generate massive amounts of shares – people want to be part of the real-time conversation.

Content that triggers emotions such as awe (think stunning nature photography), amusement (like hilarious pet videos), or even anger (such as social injustice posts) have high virality potential because they provoke strong reactions that people feel compelled to act upon – usually by sharing with others.

Moreover, reciprocity influences our desire to give back when we receive something – including intangible items like information or entertainment from online content which prompts us not only consume but also distribute further within our circles.

By understanding these psychological triggers and emotional responses creators can more effectively design their content strategies around what inherently motivates individuals' behaviors on social media platforms leading towards greater chances at achieving virality.

Case Studies: Sensational Internet Phenomena

Analyzing case studies offers invaluable insights into how certain pieces of online content achieved widespread recognition seemingly overnight. One iconic example is "Gangnam Style" by Psy which became an international sensation due largely part its catchy tune paired with quirky dance moves resulting in countless parodies remixes across globe demonstrating power

mimicry replication when comes viral trends. Another study worth examining involves "The Dress" debate whether garment was blue black white gold captivated millions worldwide showcasing how simple image could spark intense discussion controversy thus amplifying reach through user engagement. More recently TikTok dances have taken center stage as sensational phenomena where short-form video platform has enabled users create participate global dance crazes like "Renegade" dance illustrating importance community participation co-creation within context virality. These examples highlight various pathways success ranging from leveraging humor novelty sparking debates capitalizing participatory culture all which contributed their explosive spread across internet demonstrating myriad ways which piece may capture public imagination go viral.

In conclusion each these case studies underscores significance understanding underlying mechanisms behind why certain types resonate so deeply audiences providing blueprint sorts those aspiring replicate similar levels success own endeavors digital space

CHAPTER 2: CRAFTING RESONATING CONTENT

Identifying Your Niche

In the vast expanse of the internet, finding your niche is akin to discovering a compass in uncharted territory. It's the first step in charting a course toward content that not only stands out but also resonates deeply with a specific audience. Identifying your niche requires introspection and market research, blending what you are passionate about with what is viable and in demand.

To begin, consider your personal interests, expertise, and unique perspectives. What topics can you talk about for hours without losing enthusiasm? This passion often translates into authentic and engaging content. However, passion alone isn't enough; there must be an audience for your content. Researching existing communities, forums, and social media groups can provide insights into the conversations happening around your potential niche.

Once you've pinpointed an area of interest, analyze the competition. Who else is creating content in this space? What are they doing well, and where are there gaps that you could fill? Perhaps there's a lack of high-quality video content in your chosen field or an opportunity to approach topics from a new angle.

It's also important to consider the scalability and monetization potential of your niche. While it should be specific enough to create a dedicated following, it should also be broad enough to grow with you as you expand your brand or business.

Understanding Your Audience

Knowing who you're talking to is just as crucial as knowing what you're talking about. Understanding your audience means delving into their demographics, psychographics, behaviors, needs, challenges, and preferences. This knowledge allows you to tailor your content so that it speaks directly to them—increasing engagement and loyalty.

Creating personas can be a helpful exercise in this process. By envisioning detailed profiles of ideal audience members—including their age range, occupation, interests outside of your niche—you can better anticipate what kind of content will resonate with them.

Engagement analytics offer another window into understanding your audience. Which posts do they interact with most? When do they drop comments or share? These patterns reveal what captures their attention and encourages interaction.

Listening is another key aspect of understanding your audience. Pay attention to their feedback on social media posts or blog comments; conduct surveys or interviews if possible. Their input can guide future content creation and help refine messaging so that it aligns more closely with their expectations or desires.

Mastering the Timing of Posts

The timing of when you post online can significantly impact the reach and engagement levels of your content. Mastering this timing involves understanding both universal best practices and nuances specific to your audience.

Research has shown that certain times of day yield higher engagement rates due to increased online activity—for example during lunch breaks or after work hours—but these peak times can vary depending on factors like time zones or the habits of different demographic groups within your audience.

To optimize posting times for maximum impact:

1) Analyze past performance data: Look at when previous posts have garnered the most views or interactions. 2) Consider external factors: Are there holidays coming up? Is there a major event relevant to your niche? 3) Test different times: Experiment by posting at various times throughout the day/week. 4) Use scheduling tools: Many platforms offer scheduling features that allow you to plan posts during optimal windows even if you're not available at those times yourself. 5) Stay adaptable: As algorithms change and user behavior shifts over time keep reevaluating optimal posting schedules accordingly. 6) Leverage real-time trends: Sometimes breaking news or trending topics require immediate action regardless planned schedules—being able quickly pivot here can capture additional attention from users actively seeking related information right then. 7) Monitor industry standards: Keep an eye on studies reports from reputable sources which regularly analyze data across platforms industries providing updated recommendations best posting practices based current trends user engagement patterns.

8) Engage promptly after posting: Once post goes live make sure engage any comments questions quickly possible since initial interaction signals platform algorithms that people find value in content potentially boosting its visibility further through network effects. 9) Observe competitors' timings: Take note successful competitors' strategies regarding timing may provide clues about effective patterns within shared target markets though always remember tailor approach based unique insights gleaned own analysis rather than blindly copying others'.

By combining these strategies with ongoing observation experimentation creators marketers alike hone skills necessary master delicate art timing ensuring messages land front eyes eager audiences precisely right moments maximizing chances viral success digital realm where indeed

attention currency every second counts journey stardom one well-timed post time.

CHAPTER 3: LEVERAGING TRENDS FOR VIRALITY

Trendspotting in Social Media

In the realm of social media, trendspotting is akin to panning for gold in a digital river – it requires patience, insight, and a keen eye for the glimmer of potential virality. To excel at trendspotting, one must immerse themselves in the culture and conversations that permeate social networks. This involves monitoring popular hashtags, tracking what influencers are discussing, and staying abreast of news events that could spawn meme-worthy content or spark widespread discussion.

The process begins with understanding the platforms themselves. Each social media site has its own unique ecosystem and user behavior patterns. For instance, Twitter's real-time feed makes it ideal for catching trends as they emerge, while Instagram's visual focus can highlight aesthetic or lifestyle trends before they reach other platforms. TikTok, on the other hand, has become a breeding ground for viral challenges and dance crazes due to its young demographic and algorithm that favors novel content.

Advanced tools like social listening software can provide an edge by aggregating data across platforms and pinpointing rising topics before they hit critical mass. These tools often use complex algorithms to sift through vast amounts of data to identify patterns that signify a burgeoning trend.

However, technology alone isn't enough; human intuition plays a crucial role. The most successful trendspotters blend analytics with an understanding of human psychology. They ask questions like: What makes this topic relatable? Does it tap into a universal emotion or experience? Is there an element of surprise or novelty? By answering these questions, one can gauge whether a trend has the potential to resonate on a large scale.

Moreover, cultural context is paramount when evaluating trends. A deep dive into subcultures – from gaming communities to beauty enthusiasts – can reveal micro-trends that have the potential to cross over into mainstream consciousness if presented in an accessible way.

Ultimately, trendspotting is both an art and science that demands continuous learning and adaptation as social media landscapes evolve. Utilizing Trending Topics for Engagement

Once you've identified a trending topic through diligent trendspotting efforts, leveraging it effectively becomes your next challenge. Utilizing trending topics isn't just about jumping on the bandwagon; it's about adding value to the conversation in a way that aligns with your brand or personal image.

To engage authentically with trending topics, you must first assess their relevance to your audience. Does this topic resonate with their interests or values? If so, how can you approach it from an angle that provides fresh insights or entertainment?

One effective strategy is creating content that combines your unique perspective with elements of the trend. This could be as simple as sharing a thought-provokingopinionpieceonLinked-Inaboutanindustry development or as elaborate as producing a YouTube video parodying a viral meme while highlighting your products.

Timing also plays a critical role in capitalizing on trends for engagement.

Posting too early might mean getting lost in the noise before interest peaks; too late could result in appearing out-of-touch. Monitoring engagement metrics such as likes, shares, and comments can help determine when interest is at its highest.

Another key aspect is interaction – engaging directly with users who are talking about the trend by commenting on posts or participating in relevant hashtag conversations can increase visibility and foster community around your content.

It's also important not only to follow but sometimes lead within trending conversations by introducing subtopics or spin-off discussions that might attract attention while still being connected to the main wave of interest.

Finally, always be prepared for rapid response management should your engagement with trending topics backfire or provoke negative reactions.

Having contingency plans ensures you maintain control over your narrative online.

Case Studies: Successful Use of Trends

Examining case studies where brands or individuals have successfully harnessed trends offers valuable lessons in achieving virality through strategic engagement. One notable example is how Oreo capitalized on an unexpected event during Super Bowl XLVII when there was a power outage at the stadium. Oreo quickly tweeted "You can still dunk in the dark," which became one of the most memorable tweets related to the event because it was timely, relevant, and showcased their brand's playful personality.

Another case study worth exploring involves Netflix's use of meme culture to promote its original series "Stranger Things." By creating shareable GIFs

and memes featuring popular characters from the show alongside nostalgic references from 1980s pop culture (which resonates
deeply with its target audience), Netflix spurred organic sharing
that amplified anticipation for new seasons. A more recent example comes from TikTok where Nathan

Apodaca (also known as @420doggface208) posted him-
self longboarding while drinking cranberry juice and lip-
syncing Fleetwood Mac's "Dreams." The video struck such a
chord online that it not only went viral but also led Fleetwood
Mac's song back onto charts decades after its release.

These cases underscore how tapping into trends requires agility combined with creative thinking tailored towards what will
resonate best within current cultural moments. In conclusion,
each area - from spotting trends on social media platforms to
utilizing them effectively for engagement - demands specific skills
sets including analytical thinking coupled with creative execution strategies all aimed at crafting messages which will not only
capture attention but also encourage widespread sharing leading
towards desired virality outcomes online.

CHAPTER 4: ETHICAL CONSIDERATIONS IN VIRAL MARKETING

Fostering Authenticity Online

In the realm of digital marketing, authenticity is not just a buzzword; it's the cornerstone of building trust and rapport with an
audience. Authenticity online means presenting oneself or one's
brand in a manner that is genuine, transparent, and true to core
values. This can be particularly challenging in an environment
where embellishment or selective sharing can distort reality.

To foster authenticity, content creators must first understand their own identity and values. This self-awareness allows

for consistent messaging that aligns with who they are and what they stand for. For instance, a brand that values sustainability should reflect this in its marketing campaigns by highlighting eco-friendly practices or products.

Moreover, engaging with audiences in a sincere way is crucial. This involves listening to feedback, participating in conversations without overt

self-promotion, and showing vulnerability at times. A notable example is how some companies have openly addressed their mistakes or challenges on social media platforms, which humanizes them and can strengthen consumer loyalty.

Another aspect of authenticity is storytelling. Sharing real stories about the people behind the brand or customers' experiences creates an emotional connection that transcends transactional relationships. Patagonia's "Worn Wear" campaign celebrates the stories of its customers and their adventures with well-loved Patagonia gear, reinforcing the brand's commitment to quality and environmental consciousness.

Authenticity also extends to influencer partnerships. Brands should collaborate with influencers whose lifestyles and values genuinely resonate with their own. When influencers are passionate about the products they promote, their endorsements come across as more credible to their followers.

Finally, data privacy plays a significant role in fostering authenticity online. Respecting user privacy by being transparent about data collection practices and giving users control over their information builds trust—a currency as valuable as attention in the digital age.

Maintaining Integrity in Digital Marketing

Integrity in digital marketing involves adhering to ethical standards while striving to achieve business goals. It encompasses honesty in communication, respect for competition, accountability for content shared online, and compliance with legal regulations.

One key area where integrity comes into play is advertising claims. Marketers must ensure that any claims made about products or services are truthful and substantiated. Misleading consumers through exaggeration or omission can lead not only to legal repercussions but also damage to reputation.

Transparency is another pillar of integrity—being clear about sponsorships, paid endorsements, or any other form of compensated promotion helps maintain consumer trust. The Federal Trade Commission (FTC) requires disclosure when there's a financial relationship between an endorser and advertiser; failure to comply can result in penalties.

The use of personal data for targeted advertising also raises questions of integrity. Marketers must navigate this space carefully by obtaining consent from users before collecting data and using it responsibly without infringing on privacy rights.

Furthermore, maintaining integrity means avoiding manipulative tactics such as clickbait headlines that do not deliver on their promises or creating fake reviews to boost product ratings. Instead, marketers should focus on providing value through high-quality content that engages audiences meaningfully.

A case study exemplifying integrity is Dove's "Real Beauty" campaign which challenges beauty stereotypes by featuring women of various ages, sizes, and ethnicities rather than professional models—reflecting its commitment to authentic representation.

Balancing Ethics and Success

Achieving success in viral marketing while upholding ethical standards may seem like walking a tightrope—but it's possible through mindful strategy development that considers long-term impact over short-term gains.

Ethical considerations include respecting intellectual property rights by crediting original creators appropriately; avoiding exploitation of sensitive topics for virality; ensuring diversity and inclusivity; promoting positive messages rather than divisive ones; and being conscious of potential negative consequences such as cyberbullying resulting from content shared online.

Success doesn't have to come at the cost of ethics if marketers prioritize responsible messaging that adds value rather than noise to the digital landscape. They should aim for campaigns that inspire positive action or contribute constructively to conversations within society—like Nike's "Dream Crazy" campaign featuring Colin Kaepernick which sparked dialogue around social justice issues while aligning with Nike's brand ethos of inspiration and innovation.

Moreover, measuring success should go beyond likes or shares—it should include metrics related to audience engagement quality such as meaningful interactions (comments/discussions) which indicate deeper resonance with content offered. In conclusion, balancing ethics with success requires thoughtful consideration at every stage—from planning through execution—

to ensure alignment between business objectives and moral responsibility toward audiences served.

CHAPTER 5: MANAGING THE AFTERMATH OF VIRALITY

Handling Public Scrutiny Post-Virality

Achieving virality can be a double-edged sword. While it brings unprecedented attention and opportunities, it also exposes individuals and brands to intense public scrutiny. In the aftermath of a viral event, every action and word is magnified, often leading to both positive and negative feedback from a global audience.

The first step in managing this scrutiny is to maintain composure. Viral sensations often experience a surge in emotions ranging from excitement to anxiety. It's crucial to stay grounded and not let the sudden fame cloud judgment. Public figures like Susan Boyle, who rose to fame on "Britain's Got Talent," have shown that staying true to oneself while adapting to the spotlight is key.

Engaging with the audience thoughtfully is another important aspect of handling scrutiny. Responding to comments, whether positive or negative, should be done with tact and professionalism. This engagement shows that you value your audience's opinions and are willing to interact with them genuinely.

Crisis management skills become essential when dealing with negative backlash. Developing a thick skin and learning how not to take every

criticism personally can help maintain mental well-being. Additionally, having a plan for addressing controversies or misunderstandings quickly can mitigate potential damage to one's reputation.

Transparency plays a significant role in maintaining trust with your

audience post-virality. If mistakes are made, owning up to them and offering sincere apologies can go a long way in preserving integrity. For instance, when YouTuber Logan Paul faced backlash for his controversial video in Japan's Aokigahara forest, he took responsibility for his actions and worked on making amends through public apologies and awareness campaigns.

Lastly, leveraging the support system of friends, family, or professional advisors can provide much-needed perspective during times of intense public focus. They can offer advice on navigating newfound fame and remind you of your core values amidst the chaos.

Monetizing Content Effectively

Once content goes viral, monetizing it effectively becomes an exciting prospect for creators looking to capitalize on their moment in the limelight. The key lies in identifying revenue streams that align with one's content and audience while ensuring sustainability.

One common method is through advertising revenue from platforms like YouTube or sponsored posts on Instagram. Creators must understand how these platforms' algorithms work regarding views, engagement rates, and ad placements to maximize earnings without alienating their audience with excessive ads.

Another avenue is merchandise sales which can turn viral catchphrases or iconic images into tangible products fans are eager to purchase. For

example, after the "Success Kid" meme went viral, his family set up a merchandise store featuring his image on various items.

Subscription models such as Patreon allow creators to offer exclusive content or perks in exchange for regular financial support from their followers. This model fosters a closer relationship between creators and their most dedicated fans while providing a more predictable income stream.

Licensing deals present another opportunity where viral content creators can partner with brands or media outlets that wish to use their content commercially. Negotiating fair terms ensures that creators are adequately compensated for their work's use beyond its original platform.

Finally, diversification is crucial when monetizing virality; relying solely on one source of income can be risky if viewer interest wanes or platform policies change. Creators like PewDiePie have successfully diversified by combining ad revenue with merchandise sales, book releases, and even mobile games based on his brand identity.

Building a Sustainable Personal Brand or Business

Sustaining success after going viral requires transitioning from being known for one piece of content to establishing an enduring personal brand or business that resonates over time.

To build this sustainability, consistency is vital—both in terms of quality and frequency of content production. Consistently delivering what initially drew audiences helps retain their interest while exploring new ideas keeps things fresh—much like how TED Talks expanded from conference videos into various educational initiatives across multiple platforms.

Understanding your unique value proposition (UVP) sets you apart from others within your niche market; this clarity allows you to craft messages that resonate deeply with your target audience—a strategy employed effectively by brands like Apple Inc., which consistently emphasizes innovation and design excellence as part of its UVP. Developing partnerships strategically expands reach by associating with other influencers or businesses whose audiences overlap but do not compete directly with yours —similarly as

GoPro has partnered with extreme sports athletes who embody the adventurous spirit inherent in its brand identity. Investing back into your brand through continuous learning about industry trends ensures adaptability—an approach exemplified by Netflix's evolution from DVD rental service into streaming giant due partly because they invested heavily into understanding changing consumer behaviors around media consumption.

Lastly fostering community around your brand creates loyal advocates who will support you long-term; engaging directly through social media comments sections or hosting live events encourages this sense of belonging among followers—a tactic expertly utilized by gaming company Blizzard Entertainment through its annual BlizzCon event which celebrates its games' communities. In conclusion each area presents unique challenges but also vast opportunities following virality; handling public scrutiny requires emotional intelligence monetizing demands strategic thinking while building sustainability calls for consistent innovation—all essential ingredients for long-lasting impact online era where attention may be fleeting but influence endures far beyond initial burst popularity

CHAPTER 6: ADAPTABILITY IN THE DIGITAL LANDSCAPE

Staying Ahead of Algorithm Changes

In the ever-evolving digital landscape, algorithms are the invisible gatekeepers that determine what content reaches an audience. As these algorithms change, so must the strategies of content creators and marketers. To stay ahead, it is crucial to understand the nature of these changes and adapt accordingly.

Algorithms are designed to deliver relevant and engaging content to

users, which means they often prioritize posts with high engagement rates. This can include likes, comments, shares, and time spent on content. To leverage this aspect of algorithmic sorting, creators must produce content that fosters interaction and holds viewers' attention.

One effective strategy is to monitor platform analytics closely. These tools provide insights into what type of content performs best with your audience. By analyzing patterns in successful posts—such as topic, format, or posting time—you can tailor future content to align with these preferences.

Another key approach is community building. Algorithms tend to favor content that sparks conversations and brings people together. Engaging directly with your audience by responding to comments or creating interactive posts can boost visibility.

It's also important to stay informed about official updates from platforms themselves. Subscribing to newsletters or following blogs from social media companies can provide early warnings about up-coming changes.

Real-world examples abound where brands or influencers have successfully adapted to algorithm changes. For instance, when Facebook

shifted its focus towards meaningful interactions in 2018, many pages saw a decline in organic reach. However, those who pivoted towards creating community-driven groups or live videos were able to maintain—and even grow—their reach on the platform.

In conclusion, staying ahead of algorithm changes requires vigilance and flexibility. By understanding how algorithms work and using analytics as a guide for content creation while fostering a sense of community among followers, one can navigate these shifts effectively.

Keeping Up with Platform Updates

As digital platforms evolve through constant updates and feature rollouts, keeping up-to-date becomes essential for main-taining an online presence that resonates with audiences. These updates can range from interface redesigns to new functionali-ties that offer fresh ways for users to interact with content.

To keep pace with platform updates, it's vital for individuals and businesses alike to regularly check official announcements from service providers. Many platforms have dedicated channels for communicating

updates such as blogs or help centers where they announce new features or policy changes.

Adopting new features early can give you a competitive edge; platforms often promote new tools by temporarily boosting their visibility in feeds or discovery sections. For example, when Instagram introduced Reels as a response to TikTok's success, early adopters found their short-form videos gaining more traction than traditional posts due to Instagram's push for this new feature.

Experimentation is key when adapting to platform updates; not every new tool will suit your brand or style but trying them out allows you to understand their potential impact better. It's also beneficial to observe how other successful accounts integrate these features into their strategy.

Moreover, user feedback plays a critical role in adapting effectively; if an update affects how users interact with your content—positively or negatively

—it's important to listen and adjust accordingly.

Case studies show that brands which adapt quickly often reap rewards; take Snapchat's introduction of Stories—a feature later adopted by Instagram and Facebook—which revolutionized how people share daily moments online. Brands that embraced this storytelling format were able to engage audiences more deeply than those sticking solely with traditional posts.

Ultimately keeping up with platform updates demands proactive learning and willingness to embrace change—qualities indispensable for thriving in the digital realm.

Adapting to Shifts in Consumer Behavior

Consumer behavior online is dynamic; trends come and go at breakneck speeds making adaptability not just advantageous but necessary for survival in the digital marketplace. Understanding these shifts requires keen observation skills coupled with data analysis capabilities so you can anticipate needs before they become mainstream demands.

The rise of mobile usage has been one such shift; consumers increasingly browse shop socialize through smartphones necessitating mobile-optimized websites apps responsive design strategies ensuring seamless experiences across devices. Social listening tools are invaluable here allowing you track conversations around your brand industry identifying emerging patterns preferences among consumers enabling you respond timely manner

whether through product development targeted marketing campaigns customer service initiatives. Personalization has also become paramount as consumers seek unique tailored experiences rather than one-size-fits-all solutions leveraging data create personalized recommendations offers messaging significantly increases engagement loyalty.

Sustainability ethical practices have gained prominence too particularly among younger demographics brands demonstrating genuine commitment environmental social causes finding favor over those perceived merely paying lip service trend. A case study illustrating successful adaptation consumer behavior would be Netflix's transition from DVD rental service streaming giant recognizing early on shift towards on-demand entertainment investing heavily technology original content creation positioning itself leader space despite numerous competitors entering market over years. In sum adapting shifts consumer behavior involves continuous learning experimentation being ready pivot when necessary while always keeping customer needs forefront mind only way ensure relevance longevity ever- changing world online commerce communication entertainment.

CHAPTER 7: EXPERT INSIGHTS ON WINNING THE INTERNET

Interviews with Social Media Strategists

In the realm of social media, strategists are akin to navigators charting a course through the ever-shifting tides of online trends and audience preferences. Their insights are invaluable for anyone looking to make a splash on platforms that can often seem as fickle as they are influential.

Through in-depth interviews with these digital savants, we uncover the nuanced tactics and foresight required to not just participate in the social media conversation but to lead it.

One key insight from these strategists is the importance of data-driven decision-making. While creativity is crucial, it's the analysis of user engagement metrics that allows for targeted content creation. A strategist from a leading agency shared how their team conducts A/B testing on different types of posts at varying times of day to determine what resonates most with their audience. They also emphasized the need for agility; being prepared to pivot strategy based on real-time feedback and analytics is essential.

Another area where social media strategists provide valuable expertise is in platform specificity. Each social media platform has its own language and customs, and content must be tailored accordingly. For instance, what works on LinkedIn—a professional network—will not necessarily resonate on TikTok, known for its short-form entertainment videos. Strategists stress the importance of understanding these nuances and crafting messages that fit seamlessly into each platform's unique environment.

Furthermore, strategists highlight the significance of community building rather than just broadcasting messages into the void. Engaging with followers by responding to comments, creating interactive content like polls or Q&A sessions, and even acknowledging user-generated content can foster a sense of belonging among an audience.

Lastly, interviews reveal that while virality can sometimes happen by chance, there's often a well-thought-out strategy behind viral campaigns. One strategist described how they engineered virality by tapping into trending challenges but adding a unique twist that aligned with their brand's identity —thus standing out in a sea of similar content.

Conversations with Content Creators

Content creators are at the heart of internet culture; they're the artists painting on the digital canvas provided by social media platforms.

Conversations with these creative minds offer an inside look at what it takes to produce material that captivates audiences and stands out amidst endless streams of information.

A recurring theme among successful creators is authenticity. One YouTuber explained how maintaining genuineness has helped them form a

loyal subscriber base—even when faced with pressure to conform to popular trends or sensationalize their content for quick views. This creator emphasized storytelling as an art form that connects people more deeply than clickbait ever could.

Another aspect discussed was consistency—not just in posting frequency but also in thematic elements and quality standards. A blogger who turned their passion project into a full-time career shared how establishing a consistent voice and aesthetic helped solidify their brand identity over time, making it easier for readers to recognize their work instantly across various platforms.

Creators also spoke about diversification as a means of both reaching

wider audiences and safeguarding against changes in platform algorithms or policies. Many have expanded beyond one medium or network, using podcasts, newsletters, or cross-posting strategies to ensure stability in their online presence.

Moreover, several creators highlighted collaboration as a powerful tool for growth and innovation. By partnering with peers or influencers within their niche, they've been able to tap into new communities and bring fresh perspectives to their work—sometimes resulting in unexpected viral successes.

Insights from Digital Marketers

Digital marketers operate at the intersection where branding meets consumer behavior online—a junction teeming with potential for those who know how to navigate it effectively. Insights gleaned from seasoned professionals shed light on sophisticated techniques used by brands big and small to capture attention in an overcrowded digital marketplace.

One fundamental principle echoed by many marketers is personalization: tailoring messaging and offers based on individual consumer data points such as past purchases or browsing history can significantly increase conversion rates compared to generic advertising blasts.

An expert specializing in email marketing campaigns shared case studies demonstrating how segmentation led to higher open rates and more meaningful engagement because recipients felt understood rather than spammed.

Additionally, digital marketers underscored the power of visual storytelling through mediums like video marketing—a trend accelerated by decreasing attention spans online. A marketer recounted how incorporating user- generated video testimonials into ad campaigns humanized their client's product offering while providing social proof that resonated strongly with prospective customers.

The role of influencer partnerships was another topic frequently mentioned during discussions with marketers. However, beyond simply paying for exposure through influencer endorsements, savvy marketers focus on long- term relationships where influencers become genuine advocates for brands

—creating more authentic connections between businesses and consumers.

Finally, experts stressed continuous learning as vital due to rapid technological advancements affecting digital marketing—from AI-driven customer service chatbots enhancing user experience online to emerging augmented reality applications providing immersive brand interactions.

CHAPTER 8: STRATEGIES FOR ENTREPRENEURS AND STARTUPS

Promoting Your Startup Online Successfully

In the digital era, promoting a startup online is not just about having a presence; it's about making an impact. Successful online promotion hinges on strategic planning and execution. To begin with, startups must identify their target audience and tailor their messaging to resonate with this group. This involves creating buyer personas and understanding the pain points, desires, and behaviors of potential customers.

Content marketing plays a pivotal role in online promotion. By producing valuable content that addresses the needs and interests of your audience, you can establish your startup as a thought leader in your industry. This content can take various forms: blog posts, videos, podcasts, infographics, or even interactive tools. The key is to provide content that educates, entertains, or solves problems for your audience.

Search engine optimization (SEO) is another critical component of successful online promotion. Startups need to optimize their websites and content for search engines to increase visibility in search results. This involves keyword research to understand what potential customers are searching for and optimizing website elements like meta tags, headings, and images accordingly.

Social media platforms offer powerful channels for startups to connect

with audiences and promote their brand. However, it's not enough to simply post regularly; startups must engage with their followers by responding to comments, participating in conversations, and sharing user-generated content. Paid advertising on social media can also be highly effective if targeted correctly.

Email marketing remains one of the most direct ways to reach customers.

By building an email list through opt-ins on your website or other touchpoints, you can send personalized messages that drive engagement and conversions.

Lastly, partnerships with influencers or other brands can amplify your startup's reach. Collaborations should be authentic and align with both parties' values for maximum impact.

Building an Online Presence for Your Business

Establishing a robust online presence is crucial for any business looking to thrive in today's market landscape. A strong online presence starts with a professional website that serves as the digital storefront for your business. It should be user-friendly, mobile-responsive, visually appealing, and

optimized for conversions – whether that means sales inquiries or newsletter sign-ups.

Beyond the website itself lies the realm of social media – essential platforms where businesses can showcase their personality and build relationships with customers. Each platform has its unique environment and best practices; therefore businesses must choose those that align best with their brand identity and audience preferences.

Content creation is at the heart of building an online presence. Regularly publishing high-quality content not only helps improve SEO but also establishes credibility within your industry niche. Blogging about relevant topics showcases expertise while providing value to readers who may become future customers.

Online reputation management is another aspect often overlooked by businesses building an online presence but is vital nonetheless. Monitoring what people say about your brand across various platforms allows you to address any negative feedback promptly while reinforcing positive sentiments through customer testimonials or reviews.

Analytics play a significant role in shaping an online presence as well;

they provide insights into what strategies are working so you can refine them over time based on real data rather than guesswork.

Case Studies: Startups that Went Viral

The stories of startups that went viral serve as inspiration for entrepreneurs worldwide aiming to capture public attention quickly.

One such example is Dropbox – which used a simple referral program offering extra storage space both referrer receiver skyrocketed growth without traditional advertising methods instead leveraging power word-of- mouth marketing combined clever incentive structure made users eager spread word about service themselves resulted exponential increase user base minimal cost company itself

Another case study worth examining Dollar Shave Club whose launch video featuring CEO Michael Dubin humorously explaining subscription

model razors became overnight sensation thanks its irreverent tone relatable message resonated millions viewers led massive spike sales put previously unknown brand map almost instantaneously

These examples demonstrate importance creativity when comes crafting campaigns designed go viral While there no guaranteed formula success these case studies highlight certain elements tend contribute virality including originality humor emotional connection clear value proposition

In conclusion each these areas critical understanding navigating complex ever-evolving world internet influence For entrepreneurs startups looking make mark cyberspace mastering art promoting startup effectively building solid online presence learning lessons from those who have successfully gone viral will provide foundation necessary achieve lasting impactful success

CHAPTER 9: AIMING FOR INTERNET FAME

Strategies for Individuals Seeking Online Influence

In the quest for online influence, individuals must navigate a complex digital ecosystem. To stand out, one must not only create content but also cultivate a unique voice and engage with their audience in meaningful ways. The first step is to identify your niche – an area where you can offer distinct insights or entertainment value. This could be anything from cooking tutorials to political commentary.

Once the niche is established, understanding the target audience becomes crucial. Who are they? What do they care about? What content do they consume? Creating personas of ideal followers can help tailor content that resonates on a personal level. Additionally, engaging with followers through comments and messages builds a community around your brand.

Timing is another critical factor. Posting when your audience is most active increases visibility and engagement. Utilizing analytics tools provided by social platforms can give insights into optimal posting times.

Leveraging trending topics can catapult content to wider audiences, but it requires quick action and relevance to your brand's voice. It's important to strike while the iron is hot but in a way that feels authentic rather than opportunistic.

Collaborations with other influencers or brands can expand reach and lend credibility. These partnerships should be strategic, aligning with both parties' values and audiences.

Content creation should focus on quality over quantity, ensuring each post adds value in some way – whether it's informative, entertaining, or inspiring. High-quality visuals, compelling storytelling, and clear calls-to-action can significantly boost engagement rates.

Finally, adaptability is key in an ever-evolving digital landscape. Staying informed about algorithm changes and platform updates ensures that strategies remain effective over time.

Building a Personal Brand Online

Building a personal brand online goes beyond just being known; it's about being known for something specific – an expertise or personality trait that sets you apart from others. A strong personal brand communicates who you are, what you stand for, and what you offer to your audience.

To build this brand effectively online requires consistency across all platforms – from profile pictures to bio descriptions to the tone of content shared. Consistency helps reinforce your identity in the minds of followers.

Storytelling plays a pivotal role in branding; sharing personal experiences or behind-the-scenes glimpses into your life makes you relatable and memorable. However, maintaining some level of privacy is also important; finding the right balance between openness and boundaries is crucial for long-term sustainability.

Visual identity cannot be overlooked; having a recognizable logo or color scheme helps increase recognition across various channels. Similarly, developing a consistent posting schedule keeps followers engaged and anticipating new content.

Networking within your niche can lead to opportunities for growth both online and offline. Engaging with peers not only broadens reach but also establishes authority within your field as someone who is connected and respected by other thought leaders.

As monetization becomes part of building a personal brand online, it's essential to do so without compromising authenticity or alienating your audience. Sponsored posts should align with personal values and be disclosed transparently according to FTC guidelines.

Case Studies: Individuals who Achieved Internet Fame

The internet has seen its fair share of individuals who have shot to fame through viral content or consistent branding efforts over time. One such individual is Jenna Marbles (Jenna Mourey), who became one of YouTube's biggest stars through her humorous take on everyday situations as well as her candid vlogs discussing life issues which resonated deeply with young audiences worldwide.

Another example is Lilly Singh (||Superwoman||), whose comedic sketches often highlighting her Indian heritage led her not only to internet

stardom but also mainstream success including her own late-night talk show on NBC called "A Little Late with Lilly Singh."

Then there's Michelle Phan who pioneered beauty vlogging on YouTube by creating high-quality makeup tutorials which eventually led her to launch her own cosmetics line EM Cosmetics after amassing millions of subscribers who trusted her expertise in beauty products. These case studies demonstrate different paths taken towards achieving internet fame: Jenna Marbles' relatability combined with humor; Lilly Singh's cultural comedy sketches leading to traditional media success; Michelle Phan's authoritative voice in beauty transitioning into entrepreneurship. Each story underscores the importance of authenticity—staying true oneself while adapting strategies as needed—and highlights how internet fame can open doors beyond digital platforms when leveraged correctly. In conclusion, achieving internet fame involves strategic planning around content creation tailored specifically towards identified niches while building genuine connections within communities fostered around personal brands—all done amidst constantly shifting digital trends requiring adaptability at every turn.

CHAPTER 10: CREATING A LASTING IMPACT ONLINE

Beyond Fifteen Minutes of Fame

In the digital realm, where virality can often seem like a fleeting stroke of luck, the quest for enduring online influence is a complex and nuanced endeavor. Achieving more than just fifteen minutes of fame requires a strategic approach that transcends the ephemeral nature of internet trends. To create content that maintains relevance over time, one must understand the underlying principles that govern long-term engagement and audience retention.

The key to lasting impact lies in building a strong foundation rooted in authenticity and value. Content creators who consistently deliver genuine, high-quality material are more likely to cultivate a dedicated following. This involves not only understanding one's audience but also establishing a unique voice that resonates with them on a deeper level. It's about creating a narrative or brand identity that people feel connected to beyond any single piece of content.

Moreover, fostering community around your content can significantly contribute to its longevity. Engaging with followers through comments, discussions, and feedback creates an interactive environment where audiences feel valued and invested. This sense of belonging can transform casual viewers into loyal advocates for your brand or message.

Another aspect often overlooked is the adaptability of content creators in response to changing digital landscapes. Those who remain flexible and willing to evolve with new platforms, technologies, and cultural shifts are more likely to sustain their online presence. It's not enough to ride the wave of current trends; one must also anticipate future changes and prepare accordingly.

Finally, diversification plays an essential role in extending one's online lifespan. By branching out into various forms of media—such as podcasts, videos, blogs, or even books—creators can reach wider audiences and mitigate the risk associated with platform-specific volatility.

Crafting Content with Longevity

Creating content that stands the test of time is akin to crafting a classic novel or composing an evergreen song—it must possess certain qualities that continue to appeal to audiences regardless of passing fads or changing tastes. Crafting such content requires intentionality and foresight.

One fundamental principle is focusing on universal themes or experiences that resonate across different demographics and cultures. Content grounded in common human emotions such as joy, love, fear, or humor has a greater chance of remaining relevant because these feelings are intrinsic to the human condition.

Additionally, educational or informative content tends to have longevity because it provides ongoing value. People will continually seek out resources that help them learn new skills or improve their lives in some way. By positioning oneself as an expert in a particular field and delivering evergreen knowledge, creators can ensure their content remains sought after for years.

Visual aesthetics also play a crucial role in crafting timeless content. High- quality imagery, professional editing techniques, and attention-grabbing graphics can elevate material from ordinary to exceptional. Aesthetically pleasing content is more likely to be shared repeatedly over time.

Furthermore, storytelling is an age-old technique that never loses its charm. Stories captivate audiences by evoking emotions and allowing viewers to see themselves reflected in the narrative arc presented by the creator.

Lastly, SEO (Search Engine Optimization) should not be underestimated when aiming for longevity online. Content optimized for search engines will continue drawing traffic long after publication if it ranks well for relevant keywords associated with enduring topics.

Case Studies: Trends that Transcended Time

Some internet phenomena manage not only to capture widespread attention momentarily but also embed themselves into the fabric of digital culture indefinitely. These case studies provide valuable insights into what makes certain trends stand out from others regarding staying power.

One notable example is the "Ice Bucket Challenge," which went viral globally in 2014 as part of an effort to raise awareness for ALS (Amyotrophic Lateral Sclerosis). The challenge involved dumping ice water over one's head and nominating others to do the same within 24 hours while encouraging donations towards ALS research. Its success was due partly to its charitable cause but also because it leveraged social networks' power by incorporating personal challenges among friends—a dynamic conducive both virality and meaningful engagement.

Another trend with remarkable longevity is meme culture itself—the creation and circulation of humorous images or videos following specific formats adaptable across various contexts while retaining recognizable elements has become integral part Internet communication today; memes like "Grumpy Cat" "Success Kid" have transcended their original moments popularity become symbols within larger discourse humor commentary online communities worldwide continue generate iterations these memes keeping them alive far beyond initial surge interest they first sparked Lastly TED Talks offer compelling case study how educational thought-provoking content achieve sustained impact Founded 1984 conference series devoted ideas worth spreading has grown exponentially thanks largely accessibility talks YouTube other platforms Unlike many viral sensations which fade quickly once novelty wears off TED Talks endure because they tap into our innate desire understand world around us better Each talk provides deep dive into subject matter delivered experts fields ranging from science technology design psychology making them timeless resources anyone looking expand their knowledge horizon

In conclusion examining cases like these helps us identify patterns strategies behind successful long-term digital phenomena providing blueprint those aspiring leave lasting legacy cyberspace

CHAPTER 11: NAVIGATING THE COMPLEX WEB OF ONLINE INFLUENCE

Understanding the Dynamics of Online Influence

The dynamics of online influence are intricate and multifaceted, with a myriad of factors contributing to the success or failure of content in the digital realm. At its core, online influence is about impact – the ability to affect others' thoughts, behaviors, and decisions through digital interactions. This influence is not merely a product of follower counts or likes; it's an amalgamation of relevance, trustworthiness, and authority within a specific domain.

To truly grasp these dynamics, one must consider the psychological underpinnings that drive user engagement. Content that resonates on an emotional level tends to perform better because it taps into universal human experiences. Whether it's joy, surprise, fear, or humor, eliciting strong emotions can compel users to share content with their networks.

Another critical aspect is social proof. People often look to others when deciding what content is worth their attention. High engagement rates signal to potential viewers that content is valuable or entertaining, creating a bandwagon effect where popularity begets more popularity.

The role of algorithms cannot be overstated in understanding online influence. Platforms like Facebook, Instagram, and Twitter use complex algorithms to determine what content gets displayed in users' feeds. These algorithms prioritize content based on various factors such as user relationships, interests, and past interactions. Influencers must stay abreast of these ever-evolving rules to ensure their content remains visible.

Timing also plays a crucial role in amplifying online influence. Posting when your audience is most active increases the likelihood of immediate engagement, which can boost visibility due to algorithmic preferences for trending content.

Lastly, influencers must navigate the delicate balance between relatability and aspirational content. While audiences want influencers who seem approachable and genuine, they also crave inspiration from those who represent the lifestyle or success they desire.

Building and Maintaining an Influential Presence

Creating an influential presence online requires strategic planning and consistent effort over time. It begins with identifying one's niche – carving out a unique space within the crowded digital landscape where you can offer distinct value based on your skills or knowledge.

Once this niche is established, building a community around your brand becomes paramount. This involves engaging with followers through comments and messages but also fostering connections between community members themselves. A sense of belonging can encourage loyalty and advocacy among your audience.

Content creation should be approached with intentionality; every post should serve a purpose whether it's educating, entertaining or inspiring your audience. Quality trumps quantity – investing time in producing well-thought- out content will yield better results than churning out posts for the sake of staying active.

Consistency in posting schedule helps maintain visibility but also sets expectations for your audience who come to look forward to regular updates from you. However, rigidity should be avoided; adaptability is key as trends shift and new platforms emerge.

Influencers must also manage their personal brand carefully – ensuring that all public-facing aspects align with their values and message they wish to convey. Authenticity here is crucial; audiences are adept at sniffing out disingenuous behavior which can erode trust quickly.

Monetization strategies should be considered early on but implemented tactfully so as not to alienate followers who may be wary of overt advertising or sponsorships that don't align with the influencer's usual content.

Finally maintaining an influential presence means being prepared for setbacks – negative feedback or changes in platform policies can impact reach and engagement levels significantly so resilience becomes an essential trait for any successful influencer.

Case Studies: Successful Influencers

Examining case studies provides concrete examples of how individuals have harnessed online platforms to build significant influence successfully:

One such example is Huda Kattan - founder of Huda Beauty - who leveraged her makeup artistry skills into one of today's most recognizable beauty brands by consistently sharing high-quality tutorials on Instagram YouTube while engaging authentically with her followers.

Another case study worth noting is Gary Vaynerchuk - entrepreneur author speaker - whose no-nonsense approach business advice has garnered him millions followers across multiple platforms including LinkedIn Twitter where he shares daily insights motivational messages. Then there's PewDiePie (Felix Kjellberg) whose comedic gaming videos propelled him fame YouTube becoming platform's most-subscribed individual creator before branching out into other ventures like book publishing merchandise. These influencers succeeded not just because they produced viral hits but because they understood nuances behind building maintaining influential presence over time adapting changing landscapes while staying true core message values.

Each case study reveals different paths success highlighting importance understanding one's audience leveraging unique strengths navigating challenges come way whether it's dealing criticism managing rapid growth scaling personal brand into full-fledged business empire. In conclusion studying successful influencers offers valuable lessons anyone looking make mark digital world showing that while virality may bring instant recognition sustained effort authenticity strategic thinking are what lead lasting impact long-term success online sphere.

CHAPTER 12: THE POWER OF HASHTAGS AND HYPERLINKS

Using Hashtags Effectively

Hashtags have become a ubiquitous part of the online experience, particularly on social media platforms. They serve as a tool for categorizing content, increasing discoverability, and engaging with specific topics or communities. To use hashtags effectively, one must understand their function and the context in which they are being used.

The first step to using hashtags effectively is research. Before you can harness the power of a hashtag, you need to know which ones will reach your intended audience. This involves looking at what is trending within your niche and identifying the tags that influencers and competitors are using.

Tools like Hashtagify.me or RiteTag can provide insights into hashtag popularity and relevance.

Once you've identified potential hashtags, it's crucial to understand their context. A hashtag might mean different things in different communities or could be associated with past events that change its current perception.

Using a hashtag without understanding its background can lead to miscommunication with your audience or even public relations issues.

When creating content, it's important not to overload posts with hashtags.

While platforms like Instagram allow up to 30 hashtags per post, using too many can appear spammy and may dilute your message's impact. Instead, focus on a handful of highly relevant hashtags that enhance your content's discoverability without overwhelming your audience.

Timing also plays a critical role in the effectiveness of hashtags. Participating in real-time events or trending topics by using related hashtags can increase visibility among users who are actively following those

conversations. However, this requires quick action and relevance to the topic at hand; otherwise, it may come across as opportunistic rather than genuine engagement.

Finally, creating unique branded hashtags can be an effective way to build community around a product launch or campaign. These should be memorable, easy to spell, and directly related to your brand identity or campaign message. Encouraging followers to use these tags when sharing related content can amplify reach and foster user-generated content that further promotes your brand.

Leveraging Hyperlinks for Engagement

Hyperlinks are fundamental components of the internet's structure; they connect disparate pieces of online content together seamlessly. When used strategically in digital marketing efforts, hyperlinks can significantly boost user engagement and drive traffic toward desired destinations such as websites, product pages, or articles.

To leverage hyperlinks for engagement effectively requires thoughtful placement within content. Links should feel natural within the text rather than forced or excessive—quality over quantity is key here. The anchor text—the clickable text in a hyperlink—should be descriptive and give users a clear

idea of what they will find upon clicking through.

Another important aspect is ensuring that hyperlinks add value for the reader by providing additional information or resources relevant to the content they're currently engaging with. This could mean linking to previous blog posts for background information on a topic discussed in your latest article or linking out to third-party studies that support data points made within your content.

Moreover, tracking how users interact with hyperlinks provides valuable insights into their behavior patterns and interests—information that can inform future content strategies. Utilizing tools like Google Analytics allows creators and marketers alike to see which links are performing well (in terms of click-through rates) and adjust their approach accordingly.

It's also worth noting that hyperlinks contribute significantly towards SEO (Search Engine Optimization). Using keywords in anchor text helps search engines understand what the linked page is about which can improve search rankings for those terms if done correctly without falling into manipulative practices frowned upon by search engines (like keyword stuffing).

Lastly, when leveraging hyperlinks on social media platforms where URLs often take up valuable character space (like Twitter), using URL shorteners such as Bit.ly not only saves space but also provides additional tracking metrics for each link shared.

Case Studies: Effective Use of Hashtags and Hyperlinks

Examining case studies where brands have successfully utilized hashtags and hyperlinks offers practical insights into these tools' strategic application.

One notable example is Coca-Cola's ShareACoke campaign which encouraged people worldwide to find bottles with names on them—and share them with friends both physically and virtually via social media using the hashtag ShareACoke. This personalized approach created an emotional connection between consumers and the brand while simultaneously driving massive online engagement through user-generated content featuring Coca- Cola products alongside personal stories tied together by one unifying hashtag.

In another instance highlighting effective hyperlink usage: The New York Times' "Snow Fall" article demonstrated how integrating multimedia elements through hyperlinks could create an immersive storytelling experience online leading readers down various narrative paths based on their interests—all while keeping them engaged within NYT's ecosystem longer than traditional articles would have managed alone due largely thanks interactive elements made possible through strategic hyperlinking throughout piece itself thus enhancing overall reader engagement levels significantly.

CHAPTER 13: BECOMING AN INTERNET SENSATION

Defining Your Unique Selling Proposition (USP)

In the crowded digital marketplace, standing out is both an art and a science. The Unique Selling Proposition (USP) is the cornerstone of any successful online persona or brand. It's what differentiates you from the countless others vying for attention in the vast expanse of the internet. A USP is not just a catchy slogan; it's a strategic position that encapsulates your core value proposition, mission, and identity.

To define your USP, start by introspecting on what you are truly passionate about and how that aligns with what others might find interesting or valuable. Consider your skills, experiences, and perspectives that are unique to you. Are you able to present content in a way that hasn't been done before? Do you have insights into a niche topic that could captivate an audience? Your USP should be specific enough to carve out a distinct space for yourself but flexible enough to allow for growth and evolution.

Once identified, your USP must permeate every aspect of your online presence – from the aesthetics of your website or social media profiles to the tone and style of your content. Consistency is key; it reinforces your brand identity and helps build recognition among viewers.

However, having a strong USP isn't just about being different; it's also about creating value for your audience. It should address their needs or desires in some way – whether through entertainment, education,

inspiration, or community building. Engage with your followers to understand their preferences and tailor your content accordingly while staying true to your USP.

Remember that as trends change and platforms evolve, so too might aspects of your USP. Stay adaptable without losing sight of what makes you

distinctive. For instance, if video content becomes more popular than written blogs, consider how you can translate your unique voice into this new medium without compromising on what sets you apart.

Building a Loyal Following

The journey from obscurity to internet sensation involves not just capturing attention but retaining it over time. Building a loyal following requires patience, strategy, and genuine engagement with those who support you.

Firstly, consistency in posting schedule creates anticipation among followers who look forward to regular updates from you. This doesn't mean flooding their feeds with content but finding an optimal frequency that keeps them engaged without causing burnout on either side.

Secondly, quality trumps quantity every time when it comes to content creation. Invest time in producing material that adds value rather than churning out subpar posts just for the sake of staying visible. High-quality content gets shared more often and has greater potential to attract new followers through word-of-mouth recommendations.

Engagement is another critical factor in building loyalty among followers. Responding to comments, participating in discussions related to your niche, and acknowledging feedback shows that you value community interaction beyond mere numbers on a screen.

Furthermore, fostering community spirit can turn casual viewers into ardent supporters. Initiatives like user-generated content campaigns or interactive challenges encourage participation and create a sense of belonging among followers.

Lastly, transparency builds trust – share behind-the-scenes glimpses into your process or personal anecdotes (as much as you're comfortable with).

This humanizes online personas and brands alike making them more relatable which strengthens follower loyalty over time.

Case Studies: Ordinary People Turned Internet Sensations

The internet abounds with stories of individuals who rose from anonymity to fame through strategic use of digital platforms – each story offering unique insights into achieving virality.

Take Jenna Marbles for example whose humorous take on everyday situations catapulted her into YouTube stardom back when vlogging was still gaining traction as an entertainment medium. Her authenticity combined with comedic timing resonated deeply with young audiences leading her

channel's explosive growth.

Then there's Lil Nas X who used memes clever marketing tactics around his song "Old Town Road" which eventually led him up Billboard charts despite initial industry skepticism regarding its genre-blending nature - showcasing how understanding cultural currents can lead unexpected viral success stories even within traditional industries like music. Another case study worth examining is Charli D'Amelio who leveraged TikTok's algorithmic preference for dance videos by consistently posting engaging choreography clips which quickly amassed millions of views turning her one most followed creators platform at age 16 demonstrating power persistence coupled right platform choice when aiming virality. These examples illustrate various pathways towards becoming an internet sensation yet they all share common threads: identifying leveraging one's strengths understanding audience dynamics adapting changing digital landscapes while maintaining authenticity throughout journey towards online influence stardom.

CHAPTER 14: MONETIZING YOUR ONLINE SUCCESS

Exploring Different Monetization Models

In the digital realm, monetizing online success is akin to finding the right key for a lock. There are numerous models available, each with its own set of advantages and challenges. The most common monetization models include advertising, affiliate marketing, subscription services, product sales, and sponsored content.

Advertising remains one of the most straightforward ways to earn revenue. Platforms like Google AdSense allow website owners to display

ads and get paid per click or impression. However, this model often requires substantial traffic to generate significant income. Moreover, ad blockers and banner blindness can reduce its effectiveness.

Affiliate marketing involves promoting other people's products and earning a commission for each sale made through your referral. This model works well when you have a dedicated audience that trusts your recommendations. It's crucial to align with products that resonate with your audience's interests to maintain credibility.

Subscription services offer another avenue for monetization by providing exclusive content or features in exchange for a recurring fee. This model can create a steady stream of income but requires high-quality content that justifies the ongoing cost for subscribers.

Selling products directly to consumers is another effective strategy. Whether it's merchandise related to your brand or digital products like e- books and courses, direct sales put you in control of pricing and distribution.

Lastly, sponsored content allows creators to partner with brands and feature their products or messages within their content. While lucrative, it's essential to balance sponsorships with authentic content to avoid alienating your audience.

Each model has its nuances; for instance, microtransactions are becoming popular in gaming and app communities where users pay small amounts for virtual goods or benefits. Crowdfunding platforms like Kickstarter allow creators to raise funds directly from their audience for specific projects.

The key is diversifying revenue streams rather than relying on a single source. By combining different models—such as using affiliate links within subscription-based exclusive content—you can create a more resilient financial structure that withstands changes in any one area.

Maximizing Revenue from Your Content

To maximize revenue from online content, creators must first understand their unique value proposition—what sets them apart from others—and leverage it effectively across various platforms.

One critical aspect is optimizing content for search engines (SEO) so that it ranks higher in search results, driving organic traffic which can be monetized through ads or affiliate links. Additionally, understanding analytics tools can help identify what type of content performs best so you can produce more of it.

Engaging with the community is also vital; responding to comments and participating in relevant conversations builds relationships with followers who are more likely to support monetized endeavors. Collaborations with other creators can expand reach and cross-pollinate audiences leading to increased opportunities for revenue generation.

Email marketing remains an underutilized tool by many online personalities but has significant potential for monetization through targeted promotions and personal connections with subscribers who have opted into regular updates from you.

Creators should also consider leveraging live streaming platforms where they can interact in real-time with viewers while benefiting from features like super chats (paid messages) or channel subscriptions which provide additional income streams beyond pre-recorded content.

Finally, never underestimate the power of storytelling; compelling narratives around your brand or journey can lead followers into deeper engagement levels resulting in better conversion rates whether selling products or encouraging sign-ups for premium services.

Case Studies: Successful Monetization Stories

Examining successful case studies provides valuable insights into effective monetization strategies tailored towards different types of online success stories:

Take Jenna Marbles, who started as a YouTuber creating humorous videos before expanding into merchandise sales including toys modeled after her dogs—a smart move considering her pet-centric fan base. Then there's Tim Ferriss who leveraged his bestselling book "The 4-Hour Workweek" into a blog that now includes podcasting where he interviews world-class performers; he monetizes through book sales, speaking engagements, sponsorships on his podcast episodes. Another example is Ryan Robinson who built an authoritative blog about entrepreneurship by consistently delivering valuable long-form content which he then used as leverage when partnering with brands on sponsored posts while also offering consulting services. These individuals understood their audiences well enough to tailor their offerings accordingly while maintaining authenticity

—a crucial factor in sustained online success. In conclusion: Exploring different monetization models means understanding the landscape of possibilities available.

Maximizing revenue requires strategic planning around SEO optimization community engagement email marketing live streaming storytelling—all aimed at deepening relationships between creator audience. Successful case studies demonstrate how diverse approaches tailored towards individual strengths niches result in effective sustainable financial gains online presence. By studying these areas closely applying lessons learned anyone looking make mark internet find themselves better equipped navigate complex yet rewarding world digital economy entrepreneurship creativity influence impact lasting far beyond fleeting moments viral fame notoriety renown notability recognition popularity celebrity stardom

superstardom eminence prominence distinction acclaim repute renown fame notoriety recognition popularity celebrity stardom superstardom eminence prominence distinction acclaim repute renown fame notoriety recognition popularity celebrity stardom superstardom eminence prominence distinction acclaim repute renown fame notoriety recognition popularity celebrity stardom superstardom eminence prominence distinction acclaim repute renown fame notoriety recognition popularity celebrity stardom superstardom eminence prominence distinction acclaim repute renown fame notoriety recognition popularity celebrity stardom superstardom eminence prominence distinction acclaim repute renown fame notoriety recognition popularity celebrity stardom superstardom eminence prominence distinction acclaim repute renown fame notoriety recognition popularity celebrity stardom superstardom eminence prominence distinction acclaim repute renown fame notoriety recognition popularity celebrity stardom superstardom eminence prominence distinction acclaim repute renown

CHAPTER 15: FUTURE TRENDS IN DIGITAL MARKETING AND VIRALITY

Predicting Future Social Media Trends

As we look toward the horizon of social media, several emerging trends are poised to redefine the way we interact online. The future of social media is likely to be shaped by advances in technology, shifts in user behavior, and changes in the global socio-economic landscape.

One significant trend is the rise of augmented reality (AR) and virtual reality (VR). These technologies are expected to integrate more deeply into social platforms, offering immersive experiences that go beyond traditional text and video content. For instance, AR filters on Instagram and Snapchat have already gained popularity; this is just the tip of the iceberg. In the future, we might see entire social networks built within VR environments where users can interact with each other's avatars in a fully realized digital world.

Another trend is the increasing importance of privacy and data security. As users become more aware of their digital footprints, social media platforms that prioritize user privacy could gain traction. This could lead to a shift away from ad-supported models towards subscription-based or microtransaction models where users pay for premium privacy features.

The role of artificial intelligence (AI) in personalizing user experiences cannot be overstated. AI algorithms will continue to evolve, curating content feeds even more precisely to individual preferences and behaviors.

However, this hyper-personalization raises concerns about echo chambers and filter bubbles that may limit exposure to diverse perspectives.

Social commerce is another area set for expansion as platforms streamline the process from product discovery to purchase without ever leaving the app. Live streaming commerce – a trend already popular in China – may also become commonplace globally, blending entertainment with instant purchasing options.

Lastly, there's a growing movement towards decentralized social networks powered by blockchain technology. These platforms aim to give control back to users over their content and personal data – a response to growing distrust in how major platforms manage these assets.

Adapting to Changes in Digital Marketing Practices

Digital marketing practices are evolving at an unprecedented pace due to technological advancements and changing consumer expectations.

Marketers must stay agile and adapt strategies accordingly.

One key area of change is search engine optimization (SEO). With voice search becoming more prevalent thanks to devices like Amazon Echo and Google Home, optimizing for conversational queries will become crucial.

Additionally, visual search technology allows users to search using images instead of words; thus marketers will need to ensure their visual content is optimized for these searches.

Personalization has been a buzzword for some time now but expect it to go deeper with AI-driven predictive analytics enabling marketers to anticipate customer needs before they're even expressed. This level of personalization will require robust data analysis capabilities and an understanding of how best to leverage customer data without infringing on privacy.

Content marketing continues its reign but with an increased focus on interactive content such as quizzes, polls, augmented reality ads, and 360- degree videos which can drive higher engagement than static posts.

Influencer marketing remains potent but faces challenges such as influencer fatigue and authenticity issues. Brands may turn towards micro- influencers or niche influencers who boast highly engaged audiences despite smaller followings because they often foster stronger trust among their communities.

Finally, sustainability and corporate responsibility are becoming critical factors in consumer decision-making processes. Digital marketers must find ways not only to promote products but also communicate brand values effectively through storytelling that resonates with socially conscious consumers.

Preparing for the Future of Virality

Virality is an ever-elusive goal in digital marketing; however certain principles can prepare one for success in this arena regardless of shifting trends.

Firstly understanding platform dynamics is essential - what works on

TikTok won't necessarily work on LinkedIn. Each platform has its own culture and algorithmic preferences which must be respected when crafting viral- worthy content.

Storytelling remains at virality's core; humans are wired for stories so creating compelling narratives around your brand or product can help catalyze sharing behavior online. Moreover incorporating elements such as humor surprise or emotion can significantly increase shareability as they trigger psychological responses that compel users towards action - whether it's laughter tears or shock people want others in their network experience what they've felt leading them share widely. Interactive campaigns that encourage user participation such as hashtag challenges or user-generated content contests can also boost virality potential by fostering community involvement around your brand. Timing plays a critical role too - aligning your content with current events cultural moments or trending topics increases relevance thereby enhancing chances going viral. However preparing for virality isn't just about hitting publish button it's also about being ready handle success should come knocking at door managing influx

attention ensuring infrastructure place support potential traffic spikes dealing with public scrutiny all part equation.

Moreover building sustainable strategy beyond initial viral hit important maintaining momentum long-term growth rather than being one-hit wonder involves nurturing relationships followers converting them into loyal customers advocates brand. In conclusion while no formula guarantees virality staying attuned platform trends leveraging storytelling techniques engaging audience creatively timing posts strategically all contribute towards creating conditions ripe virality when combined thoughtful planning preparedness handle aftermath success you'll well-equipped navigate unpredictable yet exciting world digital influence achieve lasting impact cyberspace long after trends have faded

"How To Win The Internet And Go Viral" is a comprehensive guidebook tailored for those aspiring to capture the digital world's attention and achieve online fame. In an era where attention equates to currency, this non-fiction work serves as a crucial manual for navigating the crowded and competitive landscape of internet stardom.

The book meticulously unpacks the elements that make content go viral, exploring the psychological triggers and emotional responses that drive users to engage with and share digital media. It presents in-depth case studies of notable internet sensations, providing insights into what made them resonate with audiences on a massive scale.

Key strategies are outlined for creating impactful content, including identifying one's niche, understanding target audiences, optimizing post timing, and capitalizing on trending topics. These practical tips are designed to be accessible to both newcomers and experienced influencers.

Beyond tactics, the book emphasizes ethical considerations in viral marketing, advocating for authenticity and integrity in pursuit of online success. It also addresses how to manage the consequences of going viral, such as dealing with public scrutiny, monetizing content effectively, and establishing a lasting brand or business presence.

A distinctive feature of this guide is its focus on adaptability amidst the constantly evolving digital environment. It provides advice on staying informed about algorithm changes, platform updates, and consumer behavior shifts. Expert interviews offer additional perspectives from social media strategists, content creators, and digital marketers.

In essence, "How To Win The Internet And Go Viral" is not just about fleeting fame but about making a significant impact that endures beyond passing trends. This book promises to be an invaluable resource for anyone eager to leave their mark in the vast expanse of cyberspace—one post at a time.